The First Christmas Ever

AF584634

ZONDERKIDZ

The First Christmas Ever
Copyright © 2014 by Zonderkidz
Illustrations © 2014 by Dennis Jones

Requests for information should be addressed to:

Zonderkidz, 3900 *Sparks Drive SE, Grand Rapids, Michigan 49546*

Library of Congress Cataloging-in-Publication Data

The first Christmas ever / illustrated by Dennis Jones.
pages cm
ISBN 978-0-310-74083-4 (softcover) – ISBN 978-0-310-74086-5 (epub) – ISBN 978-0-310-74087-2 (epub) –ISBN 978-0-310-74088-9 (epub)
1. Jesus Christ–Nativity–Juvenile literature. I. Jones, Dennis G., 1956- illustrator.
BT315.3.F575 2014
232.92–dc23 2014014216

All Scripture quotations, unless otherwise indicated, are taken from The Holy Bible, *New International Version®, NIV®*. Copyright © 1973, 1978, 1984, 2011 by Biblica, Inc.® Used by permission. All rights reserved worldwide.

Any Internet addresses (websites, blogs, etc.) and telephone numbers in this book are offered as a resource. They are not intended in any way to be or imply an endorsement by Zondervan, nor does Zondervan vouch for the content of these sites and numbers for the life of this book.

All rights reserved. No part of this publication may be reproduced, stored in a retrieval system, or transmitted in any form or by any means—electronic, mechanical, photocopy, recording, or any other—except for brief quotations in printed reviews, without the prior permission of the publisher.

Zonderkidz is a trademark of Zondervan.

The illustrator is represented by the literary agency of Alive Communications, Inc., 7680 Goddard Street, Suite 200, Colorado Springs, Colorado 80920, www.alivecommunications.com

Editor: Mary Hassinger
Cover and interior design: Deborah Washburn

Printed in United States of America

---

14 15 16 17 18 19 /NGW / 21 20 19 18 17 16 15 14 13 12 11 10 9 8 7 6 5 4 3 2

The First Christmas Ever

Illustrated by Dennis Jones

Jesus Is Born

Luke 2; Matthew 2

Long ago, the king wanted to count the people living in his kingdom. So just like everyone else, two people named Mary and Joseph had to go on a journey to their hometown. They had to travel to the town of Bethlehem.

Mary was pregnant and going to have her baby soon. Her baby was very special! An angel had visited her nine months before. He told Mary that God needed her to help him, and she said yes. The angel visited Joseph too. Now they were married and headed to Joseph's hometown to register in the census.

It was late when Mary and Joseph finally got to Bethlehem.

“I’ll be back, Mary,” said Joseph. And he went to find a place for them to sleep.

He knocked on the door of the first inn he came to. “Is there any room for two of us to sleep for the night?”

“There is no room here,” was the answer.

Joseph tried another inn.

KNOCK! KNOCK!

“Is there any room for two of us to sleep for the night?” Joseph asked again.

“There is no room here,” was the answer.

But Joseph did not give up. He and Mary were tired after the long journey.

Time and time again, Joseph asked at each inn he found, "Do you have any place that my wife and I can sleep for the night?"

And every innkeeper had the same answer. There was no room. The town of Bethlehem was filled with people following the king's orders and registering in the census.

Joseph was getting nervous. Mary was going to have her baby. She needed her rest! There had to be somewhere they could sleep that was warm and safe … for just the night.

Joseph went to one more door.

KNOCK! KNOCK!

"Sir," he said. "My wife and I are tired from traveling all day. She is going to have our baby soon and needs rest. Do you have a place for us to stay tonight, please?"

The innkeeper looked at Joseph. He thought a little while and said, "I have an idea. If you want a warm and safe place just for the night, and you like animals, I have some space in the back of the inn you can see."

The innkeeper led Joseph and Mary to his barn. It was filled with friendly animals. It was the perfect place for two tired travelers and their donkey to stay.

“You are welcome to sleep in here. It’s warm. There is clean hay to lie down on and plenty of space for your donkey too.”

Mary and Joseph were so thankful. Now Mary would have a comfortable place to sleep.

“Thank you, sir! Yes, we will stay here for the night,” said Joseph.

Joseph and Mary began to settle in for the night. Joseph was feeding the tired donkey when Mary called to him.

“Joseph, I think the baby is coming tonight! We got here just in time. I thank the Lord we found a good place to stay.”

That night Mary had her little baby boy.

All babies are special, but Mary's baby was extra special! Mary and Joseph named him Jesus, just as the angel had said to. And Jesus was the Son of God!

His mother wrapped him in soft blankets and held him close.

The Son of God was born!

While Mary and Joseph took care of their new baby, there were shepherds out in the nearby fields taking care of their sheep. They were sitting in front of a warm fire, ready to settle down for the night, when they noticed a huge and shining star in the sky.

They had never seen such a beautiful star before.
Then, suddenly, something strange started happening!

An angel appeared to the shepherds.

"Who are you?" asked the men around the fire.

"Do not be afraid. I am an angel, a messenger from God," the angel said. "I have great news! A baby was born in Bethlehem—his name is Jesus. He is going to save the world from sin."

The shepherds did not know what to think. It was amazing to see the angel and more amazing to hear the good news about the Savior.

The angel said, "Go to Bethlehem. You will find a baby born in a manger. Spend some time with the new baby. Then go tell everyone you meet this good news!"

The shepherds did what the angel said. They hurried to the city of Bethlehem. There they found Mary, Joseph, and the baby Jesus.

They knew right away this was the special baby. Their hearts were filled with joy knowing that Jesus, their Savior, was finally here on earth.

After visiting with Mary, Joseph, and the new baby, they went out into the town. They told everyone they met the great news. The Savior of the world was born.

Not just the shepherds and the people living in Bethlehem heard the good news about the Savior's birth! From faraway lands came three wise men on camels. They had seen the bright star in the sky too. They knew it must mean something wonderful had happened.

And so the wise men traveled for a very long time, looking for Jesus. Finally, they met a king named Herod and asked him, "Do you know where we can find the one who was born King of the Jews? We saw his star in the sky. We have come a long way to worship him."

Herod sent the men to Bethlehem to find the child. They followed the star again until it stopped right above the house where Jesus was living!

The wise men were overjoyed! They had finally found the place they were looking for.

KNOCK, KNOCK!

Joseph and Mary came to the door. They were surprised at who was visiting them.

“We are here to welcome the Savior to the world. We are here to worship the new King,” said the wise men to Mary and Joseph.

The wise men bowed down before young Jesus and worshipped him. They knew this child was very important to all people. He was going to save the world.

Then the wise men gave Jesus three special gifts—gold, frankincense, and myrrh. These were gifts that were just right for a new king.

Jesus Grows Up

Luke 2:52

But the story was not done …

As time went on, Jesus grew up just like every other boy. He met new people, like the wise men. He went to school, made friends, and helped his mother, Mary, around their home. He even went on trips with his parents, like to Jerusalem when he was twelve.

Joseph taught Jesus how to work as a carpenter. But when Jesus was about thirty years old, he started a new job.

Jesus started doing God the Father's work—preaching about God's love for all people.

The birth of that little baby in a barn in Bethlehem had been just the beginning of something wonderful for the world.

Check out these other books illustrated by Dennis Jones!

9780310718819

9780310718802

9780310718833

9780310718826

9780310718840

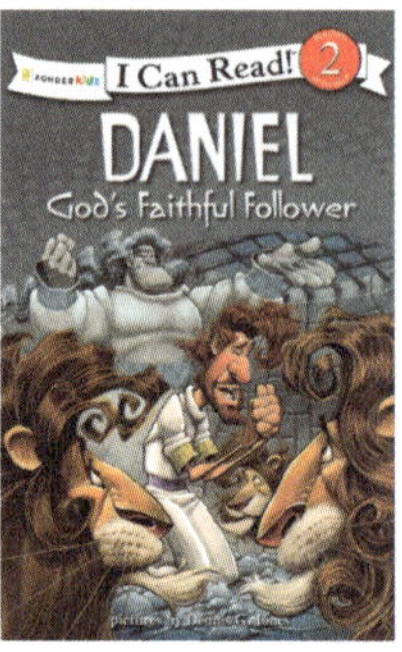

9780310718345

9780310718352

9780310718796

Available now at your local bookstore!

We want to hear from you. Please send your comments
about this book to us in care of zreview@zondervan.com. Thank you.

Grand Rapids, MI 49546
www.zonderkidz.com